Principles of A Leader

A guide to leadership Techniques and Traits

MICHAEL KASKO

In Memory of all those who served with me in the Marines and my colleagues in the corporate world of aircraft heavy maintenance.

This book is a collection of my lessons learned, analogies, favorite quotes form historical leaders, and insights into what made me successful as a leader in my career. Credit is given wherever available for those who inspired me. It is my hope that the insights and lessons in this book will help to guide and inspire leaders to reach their potential and become more successful in their careers and also be encouraged to use this information to groom future leaders.

"A true leader has the confidence to stand alone, the courage to make tough decisions, and the compassion to listen to the needs of others."—Douglas MacArthur

"If your actions inspire others to dream more, learn more, do more and become more, you are a leader." —John Quincy Adams

"There is a difference between being a leader and being a boss. Both are based on authority. A boss demands blind obedience; a leader earns his authority through understanding and trust." — Klaus Balkenhol

"The function of leadership is to produce more leaders, not more followers." —Ralph Nader

"Outstanding leaders go out of their way to boost the self-esteem of their personnel. If people believe in themselves, it's amazing what they can accomplish." —Sam Walton

"You will be more disappointed by the things you didn't do than by the things you did do." Mark Twain

ONE: Employee Retention

Leadership, Training, and Employee Retention. We begin here because if a leader cannot retain quality employees, there will be no one to lead and obviously no need for a leader. Where do you begin when it comes to employee retention? As with all issues, you must start at the top. Employees don't quit companies or their specific jobs. Most times an employee will quit this job to go to another similar job.

Employees quit their supervisors. If an employee doesn't feel needed, if an employee doesn't feel confident in their leadership, or if an employee feels they are asked to perform processes that they were not properly trained or equipped to perform, they will look for better options.

Additional issues influencing employee retention include, but are not limited to, PayScale, consistent work environment, communication, employee recognition, and yes, fair, and equal employee discipline. All qualities are controlled by a strong leadership team. Where the employee is concerned, the immediate supervisor and/or lead represents the entire company and its values.

You are part of a leadership team. You have been promoted because of your abilities and hopefully not because of a Lack-of-Options. Previously, as a member of the team you were required to focus on your training, your personal skills, and doing your job to the best of your ability while working with the rest of the team as a member, not an individual. Things have now changed.

Leadership requires a shift in some aspects of your focus. Yes, you are still part of a team, but the team you are now part of includes the leadership team. Whether you are a Lead, Supervisor, Manager or above, your focus will now shift to developing your subordinate team while working with the Leadership team.

Leadership is conducted from the front, "Leading" the way for subordinates. Always remember that your team, every individual in it, is your responsibility. Their abilities and training are now yours. You will know each employee, know their strengths and weaknesses, and use this knowledge to focus tasks based on this information.

All too often new leaders, and some seasoned leaders will assign blame when an employee doesn't perform up to the standards set for the position. They weren't properly trained, they lied on their resume/interview, they are millennials and that's just the way they are. All copouts by the leader to avoid the responsibility of training their employees up to the standards expected.

When a weakness is identified, it is your responsibility to arrange additional guidance and training to help the employee turn a weakness into a strength.

Leadership styles are a common topic of leadership training and honing your style will help you in becoming a more effective leader. However, a leadership style is not all inclusive. Different people have different personalities and while a specific style may be effective for one employee, it may be too aggressive or too casual for another. An aggressive style may cause a timid employee to get nervous and miss the point of the discussion, while a casual style may cause another employee to think you aren't serious about the issue at hand. Learn to gauge the personalities of your employees and use a style that fits the situation and the employee.

An effective leader is an influencer, never a controller. Employees who are influenced by a strong, confident, and knowledgeable leader are more productive than those with a leader who is a controller. Employees who are positively influenced will never need to be controlled.

This brings us to the pay scale. You hired this employee at a rate that you both agreed was based on their perceived skill level and years of experience. It doesn't end there by any means. Now you need to perform daily assessments of the actual skill and performance of each employee. Document all successes and failures so you will have a clear plan for moving forward with a fair annual or semiannual review with the employee. Deal with deficiencies as they happen. Don't ever let something go for several months and drop it on them at the annual review. Give the employee the opportunity to correct deficiencies and perform to a level that could justify a better compensation adjustment. This approach works better for the employee and for the company as production and quality improves in a timely manner.

Perform regular reviews of the average pay for the skill and experience in the industry and ensure the compensation is competitive. You don't have to be at the top of the industry scale, just make it harder for the employee to find a better deal elsewhere, or one that would justify the move to another company.

What about training? To get some employees into the more competitive pay ranges, you may need to train them to justify the rise in compensation. Remember, training an existing employee is easier and much more cost effective for the company than replacing an employee. Recruiting, testing, interviewing, indoctrination training, and down time between employees all take a hit to the bottom line.

At times employees may require formal training, but more often it will be your responsibility as a leader to provide on-the-job training. (OJT)

OJT is the most powerful tool in your leadership toolbox. At times you may conduct the OJT personally to provide training on things like proper paperwork handling and documentation, or to correct attendance issues. More often though, training will come in the form of you assigning a subject matter expert from your team to mentor the trainee in specific goals to help the employee become a more confident and knowledgeable member of the team.

Employees who receive regular OJT feel important. (They wouldn't continue to train me if they didn't think I was worth it.)

Many years ago, I was reading a very important book when I came across some words of wisdom that helped me considerably with this subject. Paraphrasing, it said, (referring to a farmer) "The Sower went out to sow; and as he sowed some seeds fell beside the road, and the birds came and ate them up. Others fell on the rocky places where they did not have much soil, and they sprang up immediately because they had no depth of soil, but after the sun rose, they were scorched and withered away. Others fell among the thorns and the thorns came up and choked them out. But others fell on good soil and yielded a crop.

The same analogy is true for training. A lack of, or incomplete training is like the seeds that fell on the side of the road. Untrained employees feel lost or alienated by the team and can be easily snatched up by other companies with a decent proposal.

Seeds that fell on rocky places similarly refer to incomplete or hurried training. Very little will be gained and the scorched seeds, or incompletely trained employees, will not have the knowledge required for the long-term fulfillment that is required for employee retention.

Employees trained by disgruntled employees are like the seeds sowed among thorns. The negativity passed on by these "trainers" will infect the new employees and may be very difficult to overcome.

Training in a suitable environment conducted by competent and quality employees produces the same yield as the seeds sown in good soil. Your harvest will include happier trained employees who feel that you have invested in them. These are the employees who are most likely to be with you for the long haul.

This theory is many hundreds of years old. It came from the Bible. Matthew 13:3-8

This brings us to our Processes; What do you train the employees with? Do you have specific processes that must be accomplished and a written guide for accomplishing these processes? If not, why not? Whose responsibility is it to ensure these processes are produced and available to employees?

Well, skippy, that would be you. After all you are in charge, and these are your employees. But now comes the dilemma of where to start to develop the processes that your employees will follow, and how to ensure the process will be accepted and used by employees who have been "doing it this way for years.".

Step one is to realize that you don't know everything. You are not the subject matter expert on all things in your office or shop. You hired employees to be the experts. This is where you sit down with the employee that you feel is the most proficient in each area of responsibility in your division. Task the employee to write down every step in the process for the task they are completing. Have them provide pictures or computer screen shots whenever possible.

You will take these notes and combine them into a process guide in which the employees will have ownership. Once each process is completed, sit down with the team, and walk through the process, allowing all employees to agree and/or make suggestions for changes if needed.

When all common processes are included in the guide, your employees will have a clear and concise reference for completing tasks. Everyone will be performing the processes the same way with consistent results. When an employee is out of the office, another employee can pick up the slack with a clear guide to performing the task.

Using the guide, training new employees will be completed in a more consistent and rapid manner with better results. Stress levels in the department will be reduced. Employees are not likely to look for other employment when working in a low stress environment.

To be effective as a leader, you must have a well-trained team. Task Training is important but even more important is to have a well-developed process. Task training wins battles, Process training wins wars. If your team has clear goals, and a process for achieving those goals that they can see and access easily as needed, their efficiency will increase. As the efficiency increases, Quality increases, time is reduced, and you will spend less time fixing errors. Your process guide will help with this.

Having a clear process helps but it is only part of the puzzle. Hand a task to an employee and they will clock on and get back when they can. (Or want to) Hand a task to an employee with clear direction on Tooling, Materials, and Time constraints (Task with a goal) and they will work to achieve the goals you set.

Teamwork: This is a process for issuing a task. There are many simple processes that can be adjusted and documented to ensure all team members are working together toward a common goal.

Developing a team requires consistent work environments with personnel who are familiar with each other's skills, personalities, and work styles. When these teams are consistent, they develop relationships and are more likely to help each other to be more successful.

When a facility has multiple lines of similar work, the teams naturally become competitive, and the work becomes more efficient and cost effective.

Conversely when the employees are regularly traded from team to team, the team concept is lost and the competitive spirit suffers along with efficiency and quality. Try to keep the team together as much as possible. Even if it means there will be some slow times for some employees when the workload is slow. Have the excess manpower work on tasks that enhance the work area but stay with the team. The lost time will be more than offset by the efficiency gains from maintaining a solid team.

As the workload increases or decreases, Communicate the details to the teams. Have a clear communication plan to ensure all employees receive the same message at the same time daily. Communication is another big issue that employees find extremely important in a company. All hands meetings are helpful but in some cases they only happen on a quarterly basis or less. This is too long between talks for most employees. Some will even quit in less than 3 months if the communication is poor.

The leadership team in most cases has a daily meeting with important details of the company and customers. Many times, these details are discussed in the meeting and forgotten before the leaders return to their teams. The situation is made worse when some leaders pass on information and others do not. It makes the team who didn't get the information feel like their leadership doesn't care about them. These employees are likely to look for another job.

Recognition and Discipline: When you have an employee who consistently completes their tasks ahead of schedule and/or consistently looks for additional work to help the team, what do you do? A recognition program is another tool in your leadership toolbox that will help with retention. Recognition needs to be uniform and given for true above and beyond performance. Never recognize an employee for performing exactly what they were hired to do. That is what their pay is for.

Conversely, Discipline should be used exactly as outlined in the employee manual. Issuing discipline can be difficult for the leader and employee alike. But if the discipline process is not used, employees may never realize what they are doing wrong and will not be able to correct improper activities. Additionally, the discipline program must be used equally for all employees without considering seniority or relationships. If one employee is disciplined for an infraction but other employees' actions are swept under the rug, a buddy system will be identified, and you may lose some quality employees.

Always remember to praise employees in public and Discipline employees in private. A team meeting is held to discuss the goals of the day and to emphasize safety protocol. This should always be done in a positive and encouraging tone. Start the team off on a good note. If there was an issue and a safety meeting is warranted, sometimes referred to as a safety stand down, the meeting should focus on the protocol and the correct way to accomplish the task in question. Never as a chastising of the team, especially when it was one employee who made a mistake or failed to follow the proper process. The corrective actions should be discussed with the person responsible in a private setting.

All this equates to a lower stress work environment and a job that you and your employees look forward to each day. The reward for this is employee retention and margins that upper management will appreciate. These margins are what directly affect the compensation increase percentages every year, which is another incentive for employee retention.

TWO: Perspective adapted from a former SgtMaj of the Army.

No. 1. Yelling doesn't make you Effective. Planning does.

If you're not out there with a plan every morning at 6:30, you can automatically assume your subordinates aren't either.

Planning might not be the most important thing you do that day, but it is the most important thing you do every day. The bottom line is success is determined between 6:30 and 9.

No. 2. Think about what you are going to say before you say it.

I have never regretted taking the distinct opportunity to keep my mouth shut.

You are the supervisor. People are going to listen to you.

By all means, if you have something important or something informative to add to the discussion, then say it. But do not just talk so people can hear you. For goodness sake, you are embarrassing the rest of us. Sit down and listen. Sometimes you might just learn something.

No. 3. If you find yourself having to remind everyone all the time that you're the Supervisor and you're in charge, you're probably not.

That one is self-explanatory.

No. 4. You must work very hard at being more informed and less emotional.

Supervisors, I will put it in simple terms: Nobody likes a dumb loudmouth. They don't.

Take the time to do the research. Learn how to be brief. Listen to people and give everyone the time of day. Everyone makes mistakes, even Managers, and you will make less of them if you have time to be more informed.

No. 5. If you can't have fun every day, then you need to go home.

You are the morale officer. You don't have to be everyone's friend, but you do have to be positive all the time. The supervisor is the one everyone looks to when it's cold, when it's hot, when it's raining, or things are just going south. Your job is to keep the team together. That's why you're there. The first place they will look when things go bad is you, and they will watch your reaction.

No. 6. Don't be the feared leader. It doesn't work. If employees run the other way when you show up, that's absolutely not cool.

Most leaders who yell all the time, they are in fact hiding behind their inability to effectively lead.

Employees and leaders should be seeking you, looking for your guidance, asking you to be their mentors on their career track, not posting jokes about you on Facebook. That's not cool. Funny, but it's not cool.

No. 7. Don't do anything — and I mean anything — negative over email.

You must call them. Go see them in person. Email's just a tool. It's not a substitute for leadership. It's also permanent.

You have all heard it. Once you hit 'send,' it's official, and you can never bring it back. Automatically assume that whatever you write on email will be all over Facebook by the end of the week.

No. 8. It's OK to be nervous. All of us are.

This happens to be my favorite. It came from my mother. My mom always used to tell me that if you're not nervous on the first day of school, then you're either not telling the truth, you don't care, or you're just plain stupid. [Being nervous] makes you try harder. That's what makes you care more. Once that feeling is gone, once you feel like you have everything figured out, it's time to go home, because the care stops.

Don't do this alone. You need someone you can call, a mentor you can confide in. Don't make the same mistakes someone else has made. Those are the dumb mistakes. Don't do this alone.

No. 9. If your own justification for being an expert in everything you do is your 28 years of experience, then it's time to fill out your resignation letter and retire.

Not everything gets better with age. You have to work at it every day. Remember, you are the walking textbook. You are the information portal. Take the time to keep yourself relevant.

No. 10. Never forget that you are just an apprentice.

That's all you are. No better than any other, but just one of them.

You may get paid a little more, but when the time comes, your job is to treat them all fair, take care of them as if they were your own children, and expect no more from them of that of which you expect from yourself.

THREE: A horse Analogy

It's a sunny June day in western Kentucky on a small farm. There is a barn on the hill with an old rusty tractor and some plows and other equipment in the weeds next to the barn.   Out on the beautiful green meadow a quarter horse is seen trotting across the field.   He appears to be a picture of grace and poise as we see all 4 legs working in unison to carry this young horse across the meadow and back again. A few cars stop along the road to watch the horse play in the meadow and take some pictures.

Suddenly the horse kicks up a leg at a fly on his side and he stumbles and nearly falls. Some of the people watching are seen laughing at the sight. A few minutes later another leg is out of canter and the horse stumbles again. This time some of the on-lookers stop laughing and start packing up. This goes on for a while until we see only a car or two stopping for a few minutes and then shaking their heads and moving on. There is a reason we do things a certain way. We should use the right tool for the job and follow the process, otherwise we stumble and look silly, or worse.

Down the road is the Clydesdale farm. There is always a row of cars along that section of road. People lining up to get a look and take pictures of these beautiful and graceful horses. It is obvious they are well trained, well fed, and well cared for on an ongoing daily basis. As they trot across the field, it is apparent that this is a world class animal that focuses on the job at hand. It is the textbook vision of Poise and Grace as it moves effortlessly across the meadow. The sight becomes clear as the legs are unencumbered with additional duties like the quarter horse who was trying to kick at flies instead using its tail. As the horse reached the far end of the field, we noticed the efficiency and realize the trek was completed in less time with less stress.

So how did the Clydesdale get so clearly focused while the Quarter horse is constantly stumbling? The quarter horse receives some training just after birth, but the farmer is too busy and can't be bothered to spend any more time with the quarter horse. He says, that is a quarter horse, and he is supposed to know how to trot. He has his quarter horse papers and is expected to perform like a quarter horse.

Meanwhile down at the Clydesdale farm they have a team of well-trained people who are focused on their jobs. From the leader to the assistant, to the feeder, to the Trot trainer and the cleaners, they all focus on their well-defined positions and do their part with pride. Each horse receives basic training soon after birth like the Quarter Horse. However, The Trot Trainers spend plenty of time working with the horse with repetitive training and follow-up. They don't have the Trot Trainers shoveling manure due to the cleaners not getting it done. The cleaners are well trained and never fall behind in their work. They are informed daily about what must be done and when it needs to be completed. Senior cleaners constantly provide OJT to junior cleaners. Senior Trot trainers constantly provide OJT to junior Trot Trainers.

Each Horse has a team dedicated to the training and overall performance of that horse. All of the teams have a common goal; therefor they all work to the same standards with common processes, schedules, and models. Stalls, Stables, and corrals are all set up in similar layouts to ensure they all are working towards the same goals with similar equipment.

All training is documented and performed to the same high standards. Staffing is set up to provide the support needed and ensure the staff can provide full coverage while also having plenty of family and recreation time to prevent burnout. Junior Trainers, Cleaners, and all staff are trained to become senior staff and are ready, willing, and capable of filling in when the senior staff is not available. None of the senior people blame anyone else for lack of junior staff experience because they understand that it is their responsibility to train their personnel and build a team that wants to stay and grow with the organization. The team feels important, the horse is well trained, fed, and groomed, and the showing is world class.

The result of everyone working to the same standard is a horse and/or team that everyone wants to see and one that demands a premium at all shows. NO EXCUSES!

FOUR: Philosophies of leadership.

Let's look at some thoughts to work and live by. These concepts will help you set up your leadership mindset to be effective and to recover quickly when a setback occurs. Additionally keeping these in the back of your mind will help you build a quality team that works together with you instead of just blindly working for you.

1) You will never see a U-Haul behind a hearse. You can't take it with you. Enjoy life in the day and pass on to those around you all that you can to assist in their success. Equally important as passing on material is passing on intellectual help. The adage holds true, give a man a fish and you will feed him for a day. Teach a man to fish and you will feed him for the rest of his life.

2) Have dreams but set goals. Dreams without goals are just dreams and they ultimately fuel disappointment. So have dreams but set goals, daily, weekly monthly and life goals. Achieving goals requires planning, consistency, and work, every day. People don't plan to fail; they fail to plan. Doing a lot more doesn't mean you are getting a lot more done. Don't confuse movement with progress. This is where the goal comes in. Set a goal and have a solid plan to achieve it.

3) Goals and the best plans will also experience failures. Nobody is perfect and nobody gets it right the first time every time. Embrace your failures. Each one is a learning experience that you can grow from. There is an old anecdote saying that Thomas Edison conducted 1000 failed experiments. 1001 was the lightbulb. He didn't fail 1000 times, he succeeded in learning how not to make a lightbulb 1000 times. True? Maybe, maybe Not, but the point is still valid.

4) When you achieve success, reach back, and pull someone up with you. Each one, Teach one. Don't just aspire to make a living, aspire to make a difference.

5) If you want to succeed as a leader, Surround yourself with successful people. Encourage them, Train them, support them, and you will be infinitely more successful.

6) Leave every stop in your career better than when you found it. Work tirelessly to improve your career while improving others on your way. Success is measured by how well your department succeeds when you are NOT there. If they fail when you leave, you have failed as a leader.

7) Don't make choices that are self-gratifying today. Work on goals that will promote your success in

the long run. Demeaning a subordinate today to make yourself look smarter will ultimately backfire in the future. Take that opportunity to train and encourage the subordinate who will ultimately make you look good in the long run. This will ultimately filter through the entire team fostering a culture of encouragement and success for the team and the company.

8) In the end, you will have more regret for the things you didn't do than for the things you did.

FIVE: Leadership tips.

Become an active listener

Listen very well. Don't just listen; actively listen. You must be present; you have to be in the moment, and you have to be non-judgmental. Sometimes you just must go with an idea. And the way you do that is to listen and then build on that thought.

We've learned that being a better listener makes you a better communicator. You've heard everyone out so you're able to make decisions without overlooking things. You should not be thinking of the thing you were going to say next; you should be paying attention to what's happening now.

We don't know where we're going; we only know where we've been. So, it's paramount that we all retain that information because it influences our decisions.

A lot of people pride themselves on multitasking. But basically, all multitasking is doing a lot of things in an average way.

When people are actively listening, they're retaining anywhere from 90 to 95% of the pertinent information. When they're multitasking, they may retain 40%. If you're at work running around only retaining 40% of the information, you're doing yourself a disservice, and you're certainly doing everyone around you a disservice.

Practice "yes, and . . ."

The number one rule that we have is to strike the word "no" and replace it with the two magic words "yes, and. " It's a philosophy, not a statement.

It means that you don't judge an idea. You agree with it by saying "yes," and then you add your 2 cents so that it becomes a collective idea and both people have by in to its success.

People are often "no, but . . ." There's a lot of negativity. People will always find the problem or the reason for not doing something.

But they aren't mistakes in our world; there are only disruptions from the routine. Improv forces you to solve scenarios on the fly. We're all about finding a work around and moving forward.

Becoming a "yes, and . . ." person is like going to the gym. You have to practice it everyday and reframe your brain to not go to "no" first. If it has to be a "no," so be it, but make it a considerate "no."

Embrace all ideas

One of the rules that we live by is that there are no wrong or bad ideas, and nobody's ideas are any better or worse than anyone else's. There are just high- and low-percentage choices.

The creativity comes when you can recognize that every idea has merit. What we've found is that sometimes those low-percentage choices end up being wonderfully creative ideas that we would have never come up with because we would have dismissed them early as wrong. These ideas get the ball rolling.

When you do that within your business, you develop a culture where people realize they're going to be heard and that they're not going to be judged or shot down.

Imagine how creative you would be if whatever you brought to the table, your team would build upon. There's no fear involved. The freedom to create is endless.

Empower your team

If you practice these techniques, you're honoring and empowering those around you, and they in turn will honor and empower you.

For instance, we noticed that a lot of people were on their phones before and during our show. From our perspective as the performers on the stage, we thought it was rude. But then our technical director, who sits behind the audience and runs the lights and sound, told us that he was seeing people give us five-star reviews and tweet about the show.

He suggested that instead of being angry, we should incorporate phones into the show. Now, we have people upload funny photos on our Facebook page, and we improvise from the photos.   As a happy accident to this, our social media numbers are through the roof.

When people think about the corporate ladder, they think that the way to get ahead is to step on whomever you need to step on.   But that's not how we advance. The way we ascend is by making each other look good. We pull each other up.

The relationship with your boss is one of the most important in the workplace. Your boss has the power to recommend you for new assignments, stretch goals, high-profile teams, promotions, and raises. He can make your life miserable or help you achieve your goals. Yet, despite the importance of this relationship, there are many more books on how to manage direct reports than how to manage bosses. This article explores four factors—style, context, relationship, and urgency—to consider before giving up on the relationship with your boss.

SIX: Leadership Factors.

The Style Factor

 Your boss can't seem to create a plan to save his life and it's driving you crazy. Yes, your boss may have been promoted beyond his level of competency. It's also possible—and much less frustrating to manage—if it's a simple style issue.

People are wired in different ways. Some of us can't live without action items and project plans. Others find lists to be overly constricting, tedious, and counterproductive.

Bridging the style gap is easier than it sounds. For years, assessment tools like the Myers-Briggs Type Indicator, FIRO-B, DiSC, Insights, and others have identified people's preferences and "defaults": the behaviors that they return to repeatedly, particularly during times of fatigue and stress. By gaining awareness of your own defaults, you can quickly and easily identify the gaps between the styles of you and your boss.

Common style clashes occur around a few predictable issues:
Attitude towards uncertainty: Do you prefer to respond in the moment and create as you go while your boss can't function without a plan? Or vice versa?

Attitude towards time: Are you always 5 minutes early to meetings while your boss can show up 10 minutes late? Or vice versa?

Attitude towards control: Do you like to work loosely and independently while your boss prefers to control processes tightly and review work? Or vice versa?

Information processing: Do you need quiet time to process information and think through courses of action while your boss doesn't seem to be able to function without talking? Or vice versa?

Having a conversation about style can be easy and non-confrontational. By referring to what you know to be true—that people have different orientations and attitudes towards things like uncertainty and time—you move out of the blaming trap into a problem-solving discussion. The conversation shifts from "I think you're crazy because you don't plan" to "We have different orientations towards planning. Let's talk about what we'll do to satisfy both of our needs."

This conversation should focus on a hybrid solution that makes both of you comfortable in the environment. One focuses on the details while the other sees the big picture. Daily discussions on what each see and a solution mindset with both inputs will ultimately end with a more successful operation than a separatist daily confrontation.

The Context Factor: As you enter the leadership realm, your new boss has infinitely more responsibility than you may be used to dealing with. It's time to learn how to deal with the new leadership structure at your new level.

It's easy to blame your boss for not getting back to you on time or not prioritizing your needs. You know you're calling for a good reason, but he just doesn't seem to understand that you need his help now! Before getting angry, consider the context in which your boss operates. Most leaders function in worlds of complexity. They're pulled in multiple directions. They manage diverse constituencies. They're thrown curve balls every day while being expected to keep all the balls in the air.

In this world of complexity and responsibility, your phone call is a blip on the screen, a whisper of noise amidst the deafening roar. So how do you make your important issue become his important issue? Try these techniques:

Choose your moment. You probably already know the best times to approach your boss. Perhaps it's first thing in the morning... or perhaps it's deadly to talk before he's had his coffee. In any case, choose your moment wisely, when he can focus on you and when he's fairly calm.

Plan your message. In the world of complexity, bosses are often overwhelmed by the number of problems to solve and issues to address. Break the mold by thinking through your message before approaching your boss. What is the bottom line? What is the impact on the business? What are some options you've explored? What do you need from him? That way, when you talk, you know what you want, what you need, and how to say it so that he can hear it.

Link to his concerns. What does your boss care about? What makes him tick? What are his pet peeves? What is he being called on to deliver by his bosses? Before entering his office, think through his context. What is on his mind? How does resolving your issue help address his issues?

The Relationship Factor: Your boss seems to spend all his free time with one of your colleagues. Their kids are on the same soccer team and so the two see each other outside of work. Why aren't you surprised, then, that your colleague's projects get more attention than yours? Relationships fuel interactions in organizations. The more someone trusts you, the more likely that person is to seek you out for advice, listen to your requests, and collaborate with you. It's no different with your boss. Like you, he tends to go to the people he trusts. Are you one of those people?

Often people mistake "building relationships" for becoming intimate friends with colleagues. Not true! There's no need to tell your boss about your drunken college hijinks or the details of your recent doctor's appointment. However, you do need to know enough about your boss to let him know that you understand and support him. Here are some questions to help you assess how well you know your boss:

What is your boss's family situation? Does he have children? Young or grown?

What are your boss's hobbies and/or habits outside of work? Does he ski, breed Yorkshire terriers, or grow organic vegetables?

How does he like people to communicate with him? By phone, email, in person, some other way? Which tasks does he prefer to delegate? In which tasks does he like to participate? What things can you do to help him out that he'll deeply appreciate?

Can you answer all the questions? None? If you don't know very much about your boss, it's time to start learning... and then acting on what you know. Perhaps that means covering for your boss when he picks up his sick 6-year-old or including him in tasks involving R&D, his favorite function. Then, when you need him to listen, he'll be more likely to be there for you since you've so clearly been there for him.

The Urgency Factor: And, finally, remember the story of the boy who cried wolf. He kept sounding false alarms—the wolves are here! —to see if the villagers would really come. They did, but eventually, they got tired. And when the real wolves showed up, they didn't respond to the boy's alarm, and he was forced to confront them himself. Make sure that the alarms you're sounding are real ones. Think through how you want to use your boss. Do you really want to use him for this issue? Or can it wait? Plan your time with him wisely, and you'll be much more successful managing up.

SEVEN: Recognition

Most leaders are quick to call out errors and focus on timelines and goals. This is important and must be maintained within the perspective of the project. However, many leaders are lacking in the ability to see the value of recognition programs.

When people feel valued, other positive emotions result, such as motivation and loyalty. If you truly want your organization to succeed, you must put the time and energy into ensuring that your employees feel important.

Every leader is responsible for the morale and welfare of their employees. If you want to have an effective team with the longevity to create a world class program, you need to recognize the successes of the individuals as well as the team.

Effective employee recognition and rewards can significantly improve employee engagement, which results in superior productivity, better job performance, and strong company loyalty.

This translates to better employee retention, lower recruiting costs, and a more respectable bottom line.

All staff members should be given equal opportunities to be rewarded for their efforts. Therefore, recognition should be achievable to all team members.

Employee recognition should be provided for a specific behavior or achievement. It should also be delivered in a timely manner.

Never recognize an employee for doing the basic duties they were hired to complete. That is what the paycheck is for. Recognition should be reserved for those who exceed the expectations of the job description to help the team and company to succeed.

For example, an employee comes to work every day on time for a year. Well, that is what you are supposed to do. But if the same employee were to come in early and/or stay late to complete a hot project with a tight schedule, that would be noteworthy and deserving of recognition.

Types of recognition that you can control as a leader include:

A simple Thank You and pat on the back, while simple and free, is appreciated by employees when delivered sincerely by a boss they respect.

Letter of appreciation for a job well done. These should be given in a group setting and the letter read to the team so everyone can show their appreciation for the extra effort that the employee put forth.

A pizza party for lunch. Most companies will cover the cost of this when shown the reason for the recognition. Just ask and you may receive.

As with a Pizza lunch, having some form of company logo item for recognition may be covered by the company. A coffee mug, A coin, a backpack, etc. These items take more effort to obtain, but the employees will appreciate the effort.

Employee of the month with a front row parking spot is always a big hit with employees.

Trust is built when people recognize their teammates performing well. Promote peer-to-peer recognition by creating a shout-out wall for team members to publicly display compliments and kudos to each other.

To be effective, ensure all recognition is forwarded to Human Resources to be entered into the employee's record. When the time comes to request a raise in compensation for the employee, you will have all the documentation needed to back up the request.

Types of recognition to avoid include:

Taking an hourly employee off site to lunch. While the gesture may seem sincere, the employee must clock out for lunch and if the lunch exceeds their normal lunch period, they will be losing money for every minute they are away. Not many lunches are going to make up for the hourly rate lost, especially if it reduces any overtime worked this week.

Time off for hourly employees means loss of pay for that day. So, unless you can convince the company to provide additional paid time off, don't offer a day off to your hourly employees.

All recognition needs to be consistent, fair, and without any bias.

Don't recognize only the results; recognize the growth it takes to accomplish those results. Publicly recognize the effort and call out the special determination that it took to get the task done. This will help others with duplicating the achievement. In the end, others achieve more, and the company will see more success from the success of the employees.

EIGHT: Activities
Margins, Retention, and Efficiency

Margins and employee retention are mutually inclusive. To increase margins, we need a strong and effective workforce. The strong and effective workforce provides the horsepower and efficiency to increase margins. The increased margins provide the flexibility to compensate the workforce to help retain quality workers. If both systems do not contribute, both will eventually fail.

The retention of employees that we need the most is not solely dependent on compensation. Granted, compensation has a significant effect on retention, but to understand the full cause and effect we must put ourselves in their shoes. In the eyes of the direct employee on the floor, who is this company? Who is it that has the biggest impact on their perception of our company? Who is it that can make them Love coming to work?

In years past I worked as a mechanic at an aircraft overhaul facility. That was by far the best work experience of my career. Each day as I reported to the staging area outside the control center, I was greeted by a lead. This lead made sure I and all my co-workers understood what was expected to achieve success today. I looked up to my Team Lead as someone who I wanted to emulate. Each morning at the crew meeting these leads had a crew roster with work assignments for each employee. We knew where, when, and how much work we had to complete that day. The lead explained the workload, he knew our abilities, and always had something that would challenge us. I looked forward to coming in because it was organized; the leaders were knowledgeable and focused on what was important. We had a team of mechanics who were dedicated to this line and our leader, and we competed against the other lines. In our eyes, the Team Lead was the company.

The Team Lead is the critical liaison between the mechanic and supervision. Somewhere along the line in recent history the focus departed from training and supporting the Lead. We had a lead for each skill who worked the control center constantly organizing the workflow and monitoring the budget. (Lead in training to be a supervisor). We also had an assistant lead for each skill who assigned tasks, monitored progress, and ensured the mechanics had everything they needed on the floor. (Assistant Lead in training to be Lead). Supervisors train and mentor the Team Leads in time-management techniques and people skills. We didn't have shortages of leadership because the leadership was mentored and had increasing responsibility as they progressed.

Training the Team Lead in the how and why of time management will go a long way to improve the efficiency of the project and the perception of the company to the employees. Leads get trained by their supervisors. Supervisors get trained by their managers. We have seen some training efforts in recent years, but it is a couple hours in a class then back to the floor and business as usual. A comprehensive training program of train the trainer with maintenance supervision will provide a baseline for the future. Training in the art of time management, people skills, managing employees clocking in, ensuring employees clock out, and Monitoring employee efficiencies helps to create a stable, organized work environment. A qualified and well-trained Lead is key to employees having confidence in the company they work for.

To be effective, the training requires follow-up, coaching, OJT, and consistency. As a technician is loaned to another line, the process needs to be similar. Having different basic processes from line to line and lead to lead is inefficient. Standardized Crew rosters and assignments for the next day need to be filled out by the Leads as directed by the Supervisors and Managers before leaving for the day. This sets the stage for an organized and efficient start for the next day.

Employees plan careers with organized and efficient processes. Confidence in their lead, consistent processes, and an environment organized around teamwork and friendly competition. This sets the stage for employees who want to stay and be part of something bigger than themselves.

NINE: Never Retreat.

When deciding how to Lead, a firm commitment to the goal is usually the best approach. We make plans and review the plans with our teams, but all too often we give them an option, or a get out of jail free card with a Plan B. This philosophy invites a less than full commitment and a way out even before one may be necessary.

In 1519, a Spanish conquistador named Hernán Cortés embarked on a mission to conquer the vast Aztec Empire. With only a few hundred men, he faced an empire that numbered in the thousands. His soldiers, already fearful of the overwhelming odds, could easily have chosen to retreat. They could have looked to their ships as an escape, a way to turn back and return to the safety of the familiar.

But Cortés had a brilliant plan. He issued the command: "Burn the boats."

Soon the opportunity to retreat was removed. The soldiers had no choice but to press forward, to fight with all their strength. The only option left was victory. This act of burning the boats wasn't about destroying ships. This was about burning the mindset of failure, the alternative to retreat, and the desire to look back.

As leaders, we remember these examples and utilize the lesson to help us ensure success.

Often, when faced with challenges, we set up a safety net. Why do we let ourselves dwell on the "what-ifs," the backups, and/or the security of old habits? True leadership, the kind that inspires and transforms, requires us to burn those figurative boats.

Fully committing to a vision, removing the option to go back, we set ourselves and our teams on a path to success. This is the essence of leadership, stand firm in the face of uncertainty, trust in your ability to adapt and grow, and lead others to do the same.

Consider the projects you're currently leading/working on, the teams you're responsible for. Is there a boat you're holding on to? Is there a part of you that still looks back at a time when things were easier, or are you holding onto a plan B, just in case? What if, instead, you burned that boat? What if you committed your team to moving forward, no matter what?

Burning the boats is about confidence—belief in the mission, confidence in your people, and confidence in yourself. It's about removing excuses and establishing a singular focus on success. It's about making the bold decision that there is no turning back, no giving up.

The only way is forward!

And that's the spirit I encourage all of you to adopt today. Let's embrace the challenges before us with the courage to burn our boats. Let's show those we lead that we are committed, that we believe in our shared mission, and that no matter what obstacles we face, we will find a way to succeed—because we've left ourselves no other choice.

So, let us go forward with confidence, knowing that with every step we take, we are building a future that demands the very best of us.

There's an old quote that reads 'don't look back, you're not going that way.' It's a simple motivational thought brought about to encourage leaders to keep pressing forward. It carries new meaning now, as we realize there is no going back to pre-2020 "normal."

True, things changed through and following the pandemic of the 2020's. Some things will never change back. But there is another old quote that holds equal relevance. "Those who ignore history are bound to repeat it". While some things may never be the same, the lessons of the past as well as the plans and processes that were successful may be just as valid today.

As a leader you have the responsibility to study the old and the new and use all available information to make the best possible decisions to ensure the success of your team and the company.

Blindly moving forward with only the perceived "relevant" information is an invitation to fail or at least succeed with a lower level of success and profit for your company. The terms old and obsolete are not mutually applicable. The company is still in business with its current level of success because of the "Old Ways". They worked before and some may still work, especially when combined with new ideas. So, don't discount the old just because it's old.

TEN: Principles of leadership.

Let's sum it all up with the principles that make a good leader.

1. Lead by example

Set the example. A good leader influences and nurtures their team. Successful leaders show employees how it's done and encourage everyone to contribute to achieving the goal. Employees won't enthusiastically follow a leader who doesn't perform to the same standards as he or she demands from them.

2. Leadership is about people

Effective communication and engagement with your team are crucial to successful leadership. Without clearly communicating your vision, leading can be tricky. As a leader, aim to build strong relationships with every team member, from top-level executives to those in lower-level positions. These relationships are professional and personal. You don't need to spend time with employees away from work to build relationships. Work on improving your interpersonal skills, and your ability to influence those around you in a positive way.

3. Embrace change

Renovation is a crucial component of any leadership approach. For successful change, people must understand your goals and their role in achieving them. Timing of change is equally important as the change itself. When a goal is set, make every effort to follow through to its conclusion. Changing a process or goal should be done and communicated with the team before the task is initiated to reduce confusion.

4. Understand the value of listening

While voicing your goals and dictating jobs, always remember that it's just as important to listen to your employee's input. Employees might uncover valuable insights that can enhance your leadership. Leaders don't need to agree with everything they hear, but they should strive to understand it. Implementing an employee's idea will help the process as well as encourage solution thinking for your team.

5. Admit mistakes

We all make mistakes, but it can be an asset for other people to see a leader admit their mistakes, since this makes you relatable. Mistakes can show you where you went wrong and how you can improve in the future. An intelligent leader learns from each mistake as well as success and uses these references to teach employees what areas need attention. Leaders who take accountability for mistakes earn their employee's respect.

6. Develop your skills

To lead effectively you will need to be able to recognize subtle issues in the way your team performs. To be a great leader you need to work to develop your personal skills in the area that you are responsible. Ideally a leader would be promoted from within the same skill field. However, that is not always possible. In that case as a leader of a new area of responsibility you will need to spend time developing your skills to fully understand what your team members should be doing daily. A blind leader is often worse than no leader at all.

7. Work together to achieve more

Realize up front that you don't have all the answers. Collaboration involves working with others to share information, strategies, and successes. Cooperation and collaboration can occur between organizations while still maintaining beneficial competition. This is an opportunity to leverage these benefits to achieve peak success.

8. Have real ideals

Successful leaders have a vision and values that they use to inspire their followers and motivate them. Values are important, and they show that you're a credible leader. Employees appreciate working in a friendly team, having flexible working hours and maintaining a job that makes them feel like they're making a meaningful impact on their community. People typically want to work with a leader who understands their values and needs and has authentic values they follow themselves.

9. Help to develop future leaders

Leaders are measured in part by what happens while they are away. This summer you go on vacation, what happens to your goals and priorities? Did everything fall apart without you? If you believe this means they can't live without you, you are likely already on the list of leaders to be replaced. If you go on vacation and your second in command picks up the ball and ensures all priorities and goals are achieved, you have shown that not only can you get it done, but you also have team building skills that are focused on the success of the organization. The organization can benefit from having a pre-established plan that leaves no gaps where people have no one to guide them. When employees learn how to become leaders, they take ownership of their work and become more reliable.

10. Authenticity

Being genuine and true to who you are is necessary to success in any role. As a leader, you must personify your best self. An effective leader who is focused on motivating and inspiring those around you is essential. Your skill is not enough; people need to trust your character and connect with you, otherwise they will not be willing to take risks with you. Seek feedback from peers. Employees talk to each other and usually with one level above them. They will share their view of the leadership that they deal with. Be open to receiving feedback from others and view it as an opportunity to improve. This should be done in an atmosphere where you can remain open without becoming defensive.

Start by asking for feedback from peers to get some sense of what I should keep doing, start doing, and stop doing. Don't dwell on the negative, request ideas on how to make subtle changes to turn it around without appearing to become something disingenuous. Employees will see right through a fake persona.

We have all seen a leader who thinks leadership is accomplished by yelling at employees to let everyone know who is in charge. If you are yelling at employees, ask yourself if this is how you interact with your friends and family. If it's not, why would you do it at work? Employees don't give 100% to a leader who is putting on a fake persona. Employees need a leader who is real, nurturing, and has the best interests of the employees, and company in mind. Find a way to lead with a focus on developing a team with encouragement and a process to reward excellence while minimizing the effects of negativity when there is an occasional hiccup in the process. When something goes wrong, remain calm, pull your team together and calmly ask, what can we do to fix this and what are we going to do to ensure it never happens again. A team that is involved in the cure is much more likely to prevent a reoccurrence of a similar mistake.

Finally, don't be afraid of change. New processes, new computer programs, and reorganization are all a fact of life. When a change comes down, gather your team and get everyone involved in making the change together. Every change will require a change in your "Normal" processes. Be sure to get with your subject matter experts and involve every skillset in the adjustments necessary to make the change. A good rule of thumb is to have the experts write down a detailed process to define the new steps required to make the change. This can be put into a process guide and used as a tool to ensure everyone on the team has a written process to refer to while the change is still new. This prevents mistakes and lets the team know that you are focused on their success in a positive way.

Becoming a great leader is an excursion of constant learning and growth. It's a process that thrives on accepting challenges, seeking feedback, promoting connections, and developing understanding. Develop the mindset, behaviors, and connections that allow you to accept challenges and opportunities and do exceptional things.

Eleven: In Closing.

From the Center for Creative Leadership:
Leadership is often described by what a leader does or the capabilities they have. Yet while the skills and behaviors of individual leaders are important, the true meaning of leadership is about what people do together. Said another way, everyone in an organization contributes to leadership.

So, what is leadership, really?

Based on our decades of pioneering research and experience, we define leadership as a social process that enables individuals to work together to achieve results that they could never achieve working alone.

Remember that a Leader is leading a team and every member of the team, from the newest employee to the most experienced, is an important part of the machine. Treat all with respect and they will do the same for you. Now go build and maintain your machine.